HARRY JACKSON

The Artist

photo by Christopher Bird

HARRY JACKSON

Monograph — Catalogue
by Frank Getlein

KENNEDY GALLERIES, INC.

Founded 1874 by H. Wunderlich
20 East 56th Street
New York, N. Y. 10022

Pony Express

A man, a horse, a gun in hand
a high moment in the saga of the American frontier.

You hear the beat of hooves on hard-packed dirt.
You feel the surrounding air of Western heat. You share the
rhythm of pulse and breath of man and horse riding,
running, racing as a single creature across the plain from
St. Joe to Sacramento. You smell the dust, the leather, the sweat
of man and beast, and, in a moment, the acrid tang
of gunsmoke — and hear the single, precise report of the
carefully aimed and squeezed off round.
This is the Pony Express, that brief experiment in mail
service — it lasted but eighteen months; its record time
of seven days, 17 hours was set carrying the text of Lincoln's
First Inaugural Address; an early rider was Buffalo Bill Cody,
the man who, as much as anyone, made the West a
permanent part of the American consciousness.
For all its brief duration, the Pony Express Service left
a deep imprint on American history as it is remembered
by Americans. To this day there are grumbling patrons
of the Post Office who swear that government department
has never attained the standards of speed set by the
private enterprise Pony Express; and to this day, more
significantly, the emblem worn by U. S. postal employees
and emblazoned on their stationery is that of the man
bent forward on the galloping horse. If there was ever a courier
worthy of the boast that neither rain nor snow nor
dark of night could stay the swift completion of the
appointed round, it was the rider of the Pony Express.
The sculpture, painted, or in the more familiar form,
patinaed, is the work of Harry Jackson, the most masterful
artist now working in the western tradition of Charlie Russell
and Frederic Remington. A native of Chicago, Jackson went
West as an adolescent and has never really left the big
country despite some years as a successful abstract painter
in New York and despite his residence in Italy of the last
decade or so. He returns to Wyoming at least once a year and
regards his work as the natural expression
of his youthful life as a cowboy.
Jackson paints his sculpture for the same reason the Greeks
and the medievals did: that's the way things are in life, colored.
The age-old tradition of painted sculpture went out in
the Renaissance, when the sculptors of the day began studying
newly unearthed bronzes and marbles of classical antiquity.

**Modeled in wax, cast in bronze, painted in careful,
loving detail, Harry Jackson's " Pony Express " is technically
in a tradition as old as art, the painted sculpture
of the Greeks, the Romans, and the Middle Ages.**

DETAIL

"Pony Express" is also a late expression of the equestrian tradition in sculpture, a noble lineage that embraces the centaurs of the Parthenon frieze, the bronze horses of Constantinople now above the porch of St. Mark's in Venice, the statue of Marcus Aurelius, the Colleoni monument, the ruined project of Leonardo, the Robert Mills "Jackson" in front of the White House, and the bronzes of Remington and Russell from the West that Harry Jackson, too, has made his own.

PONY EXPRESS, 1967,
BRONZE 21 × 14 × 18¹/₂

Study, 1966, pencil on white paper 34 × 24¹/₂

SKETCH, 1963, PENCIL ON LINED YELLOW PAPER 8 × 8

↑ PONY EXPRESS SKETCH, 1963, BRONZE, FIRST VERSION → 10³/₄ × 13 × 7

Beneath the faithful realism of the surface of the Pony Express rider lies a detailed study of the technical, abstract problems of any equestrian sculpture. These are studied and solved by Harry Jackson in sketches in charcoal, ink and pencil, and in modeled wax, cast in bronze. The basic masses, the bony protuberances and hollows of the skull-like sketch above appear complete in the finished sculpture.

PONY EXPRESS, HEAD STUDY, 1965, BRONZE $3^1/_2 \times 2^3/_4 \times 3$

These pieces, found in the sea and under the ground, had been painted when they were made, but after centuries in salt water or in chemically rich earth, the colors had vanished, leaving the satisfying textures of the stone and the metal. The whole problem in the history of taste is something like the problem of the Venus de Medici in the Louvre, the girl without arms. We are accustomed to this amputated figure, as we are to many other surviving fragments of antiquity, as a fragment. We accept the head, torso, legs as a unified whole, even though it is clear enough that no Greek ever carved such a mutilation and set it up as finished. For five hundred years we have accepted unpainted stone and metal, and it has added enormously to the values we find in sculpture, but it is unfortunate when that acceptance deprives us of the different values of painted sculpture.

The faithful and detailed realism of the finished painted bronzes of Harry Jackson begin with sketches in charcoal or pen and ink of the roughest, loosest sort. These blocked out arrangements of mass and motion tell the artist the mechanics of his vision, the " flesh " that the word must be made. These drawings led to the bronze sketch opposite,

9

a loose, almost impressionistic, small sculpture, and the independent treatment of the rider's head on page 9. The head, seen in three views, strikingly reveals the skull beneath the skin, a death's head in a Stetson. This approach constantly reminds the sculptor of what it is that lies behind the flashing vision of the rider, a solid grasp of human and equine anatomy and a realization, based on long observation and on years of riding horses " Hell for Leather. " When a good man is on a good horse their immensely complex motions quickly fuse into a single system.

STUDY, 1968, EGG TEMPERA ON PAPER 16 × 12¹/₂

These early tempera sketches and bronze studies, the first sign of a new idea, often with supporting armatures showing, crystallize the vision for the artist and set the relations between the two moving bodies. The uncluttered spontaneity of these first sketches holds a pure vitality, and through them one can almost touch the act of artistic creativity. When they are as successful as these they contain a beauty that makes them most valuable works in their own right.

←Pony Express, sketch, 1968, 2nd version ↑ 19¹/₂ × 13¹/₂ × 10

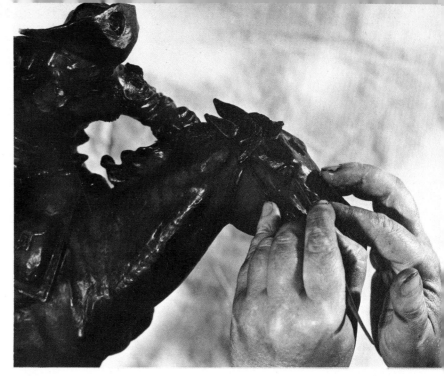

The sketches, finally,
are translated into a wax original by the artist.
At this point, inspiration and the experience of life
give away to patiently acquired
skills and the experience of making art.
Heated tools (right) work the wax form (right, above).
After the wax has been " lost "
in the traditional process, the bronze is cast in
its mold (page 13), then, after cleaning and finishing,
it is painted by the artist in delicate
and muted colors, softened further by Western dust.
The molds for bronze casting are encased
in thick drums of protective material which in turn
are held in sand inside a metal fence,
all designed to withstand the great pressures generated by
the heat and the vapors of the molten metal.

This fusion is what Harry Jackson captures superbly in his paintings and bronzes of mounted men. In art, as in life, the whole is always greater than the sum of its parts. The mounted man, in history as in art, has always been more than just the total worth of a horse and a man. For some years, Harry Jackson has been seeking and finding and making art out of that extra quality that comes in the fusion. Jackson came to the West and to the art of the mounted man all the way from his birth in 1924 in Chicago, that ultimate capital of the " cow-country. " There he realized two things very early: his natural bent for art and his utter fascination with the idea, the vision, of a man on a horse. His estranged father had been horseback in World War I and, on his occasional visits home, he took the boy to the 124th Field Artillery armory two blocks away, where they watched the polo team practice. And there, at age 5, young Harry began to ride and draw horses.
He has saddle horses in Wyoming and Italy, and his 2 year old son Matthew has been horseback, firmly held in his father's or mother's arms, since he was one month old. At about the same time of the armory visits, a great aunt, seeing his talent, began taking him to the Chicago Art Institute, and enrolled him in the weekly children's class. At grammar school, where he did little else well, he was the school artist, drawing the covers for the paper. " That's all that got me through, " he recalls. A cousin gave the boy a Hoot Gibson cowboy suit — " hat, chaps, lariat, gun, the works " — for Christmas, and the West became Harry's obsession. He haunted the private Harding Museum near his school, which owned many Remington bronzes. His mother ran a lunchroom near the stockyards and the boy passed a lot of time leaning on the counter, drawing the cattle traders and cowboys who ate there. Over those same early years, he collected some 3,000 toy soldiers of lead and papier-maché. With paint, tin, adhesive tape and bits of tiny chain, he made them into types from British-Indian Regiments, based upon extensive research. While his passionate, haphazard, self-education in art proceeded, his formal education decayed at the same pace.

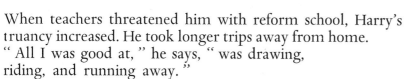

When teachers threatened him with reform school, Harry's
truancy increased. He took longer trips away from home.
"All I was good at," he says, "was drawing,
riding, and running away."
At 13 he ran away to New York, to the British Library
of Information, to check on the correct uniform details of India's
Northwest Frontier troops. At 14, inspired by Charles
Belden's *Life Magazine* photos on Wyoming's Pitchfork Ranch,
he lit out for that destination and, incredibly, made it.
Clayton Burke and Sam Decker gave him a job in Cody's
Diamond Lumber Yard, but he soon moved on to chore
boy for Earl Martin on the Bradford Ranch that first year.
There the city runaway "wrangled horses, milked two cows,
built fence, and hayed for Ned Frost across the valley."
And loved it. He became a ranch hand on Gene Phelps' Z-T
in Meeteetse, and finally cowboyed with the round up
wagon on the famed Pitchfork he'd first seen in the

Life article. He rode with Cal Todd, Oliver Bakken, Jack Rhodes, Sid and Jack Nelson, Dick Curtis, and many more good men. " Cal and I pardnered up. He's been a friend for nearly 30 years and the Pitchfork is still home to me. " When he was 18 in 1942 he moved from the cow-camps to the Marines and became an " Official Combat Artist " because of his powerful war drawings. From there he entered into the emerging world of abstract N. Y. painting. But Meeteetse was and still is home, though he lives and works in Italy, where he has set up his own workshop-studio. Jackson started his own studio-foundry on the sound principle that if you want anything done well, do it yourself. One of the underlying and unrecognized reasons for the prevalence of junk sculpture, plastic sculpture and even light sculpture in America today is that the facilities for bronze sculpture are all but non-existent outside the New York area, and severely limited there. In Italy, in contrast, there are art foundries all over the country. There is a concentration of them in the small coastal towns near the famous marble quarries at Carrara, with five in Pietrasanta. In 1958, while working on a major mural commission, the artist decided to model the scene as a sculpture and paint his canvas from the model, an ancient studio practice now fallen into disuse. He had his models cast in bronze at Pietrasanta and formed an association with a foundry there. After several years, the quality of the foundry work declined. Jackson bought some land in neighboring Camaiore and built a large studio, a workshop and minimum living quarters for himself and his wife. The foreman of the old foundry joined him and gradually they added other workers and now he has a crew of eight, including himself. He is legally an " artisan-proprietor, " a title the Italian government awards to few Italians and almost no foreigners. Jackson's foundry casts only his own works, except as an occasional favor to friends, such as Thomas McGlynn, O. P., and Thomas Hart Benton, or Jacques Lipchitz whose villa is on a nearby mountain top. By maintaining total, personal control over every step of the process, Jackson keeps his finished sculpture faithful to the vision that begins it.

In the foundry-shop of Jackson's Italian studio (opposite page) skilled artisans under the eye and hand of the artist and his foreman, Ivo Ricci (lower left and right), make the master molds for " lost wax " casting from Jackson's original wax sculptures and with equal care perform the work of chasing and finishing the final bronze casts and realizing the telling details, like the lariat and reins (opposite), from the " Cowboy's Meditation " (page 58). Above, the " Pony Express " was conceived as a model for an 18-foot monument to be executed. The artist models this new version, 3 feet high, to be cast in a small edition.

15

"River, Road and Point"

A work in progress

The painter in his Camaiore studio in front of his mural-in-progress, "River, Road and Point" for the new Fort Pitt Museum in Pittsburgh. This view shows about half of the 56 foot wide painting, starting, on the left, with George Washington's expedition, led by an Iroquois guide, and culminating in a battle of the French and Indian War, to the right of the artist. On the right, at the very edge of the photograph, the pioneers make the " corduroy road " of logs, over which the British troops advance.

From Wyoming, or even from Chicago, Pittsburgh is decidedly Back East. But it was the crucial Western frontier before our American Revolution. The frontier war, in which George Washington served as a Lieutenant Colonel, we call the French and Indian War, after the enemies, although the British and British colonists had their own Indian allies. At issue was nothing less than the fate of the continent, whether a British culture or a French should stretch across America. The war insured that this country would be English-speaking. It gave Canada and Florida to England. The war involved a good deal of Europe, the Caribbean and India. The very center of the nine year struggle, however, its beginning, its end and its real reason, was the point of land where the Allegheny and Monongahela rivers meet to form the Ohio, the point that is now downtown Pittsburgh. The French claimed that their discovery of the Mississippi gave them dominance over all the land drained by the great river, roughly from the Appalachians to the Rockies.

By mid-eighteenth century, their trappers, traders and missionaries were filtering along the waterways south from the Great Lakes into what are now Ohio, New York, and Pennsylvania. Meanwhile, west from Virginia, British colonials were settling, building roads, trapping and trading with the Indians. Conflict was inevitable. When it was over, not only was America British, but the stage was set for both the American Revolution and the French Revolution. To commemorate this vitally important series of events, a Pittsburgh foundation acquired the land of the point for a park to contain a museum. In the museum was to be placed an heroic mural depicting the French and Indian War. Harry Jackson was awarded the commission to paint this challenging mural. Following his usual procedure, Jackson began with small sketches of the overall scene, a sequence of eight hinged panels, each 12 ½ feet high, which, when mounted in place, would blend together as a single, uninterrupted flow. The transitions between the scenes are trees, which were everywhere in that forest war. Jackson has composed such disparate elements as the wild animals of the area, the Indians, and European colonization, the coming of the trapper, the French Jesuits, the waterways they dominated as opposed to the sturdy British log roads, explorers, and, at the center, an allegorical battle between the British and Americans against the French, with the Indian allies of both sides, the scene framed by a thoughtful Highlander loading his musket and a French allied Algonquin chieftain, his aide holding aloft a captured British helmet. The painted bronze sculpture of the Frontiersman on page 18 and 19 was created as a model for one of the mural's figures, but when each detail

IROQUOIS GUIDE, 1968, PAINTED BRONZE 19¹/₂ × 13¹/₂ × 10

Extracted from the sketch of the mural for Pittsburgh, the Iroquois guide was modelled in wax and cast in bronze by Harry Jackson to serve as a model for the mural. Painted bronze includes snow on ground and on the moose hide moccasins.

FRONTIERSMAN
HARRY JACKSON

Among the principal characters that Jackson chose to sculpt and color as models for the mural painting, was the "Frontiersman," his hide clothing muted with forest dust, his sharp Scotch-Irish face as if carved with an axe.

←Frontiersman, 1967, painted bronze 20 × 18 × 10

and texture is painted with stark honesty in its actual color, it, like all of Harry Jackson's painted bronzes, becomes something more, a most vital and satisfying reconfirmation of the high and ancient art of realistically painted sculpture. The patined *Frontiersman*, a page 21, reveals, in the reverse view, the results of Harry Jackson's patient research, the drive that first showed itself in his regiments of toy soldiers. The weapon is right, the axe, the powderhorn are right, the Indian sash — the true, original coonskin cap — are right. In patina as in paint, there is the feel in the home-tanned buckskin and of the crude, line-camp methods that made the stiff skin supple. This is "Leatherstocking," destined to be, about two generations later, the first historical hero of the new Republic. But the research is never an end in itself. The accurate detail is secondary to the four-square, planted feet, the sturdy, straight back, the professional sighting down the barrel, the stand of the frontiersman against the enemy who would dare call him. In the mural the Frontiersman is a central, anchoring figure. In bronze too, he stands immovable, resisting, permanent in the West.

Frontiersman, detail

The Iroquois guide of the Washington expedition is here seen in patinaed rather than painted bronze. Jackson's research revealed this peculiar, toed-in way of walking among the Woodland Indians in the eighteenth century.

The turn of the body expresses the constant vigilance of the Woodland people. The leaning of the head into the blanket not only records the winter temperature; it also expresses the blending of the Indian into his environment that was typical of the Woodland folk and had meaning both instinctive-tactical and deeply spiritual.

IROQUOIS GUIDE, 1967, BRONZE 19$\frac{1}{2}$ × 13$\frac{1}{2}$ × 10

Frontiersman, 1965, bronze 20 × 18 × 10

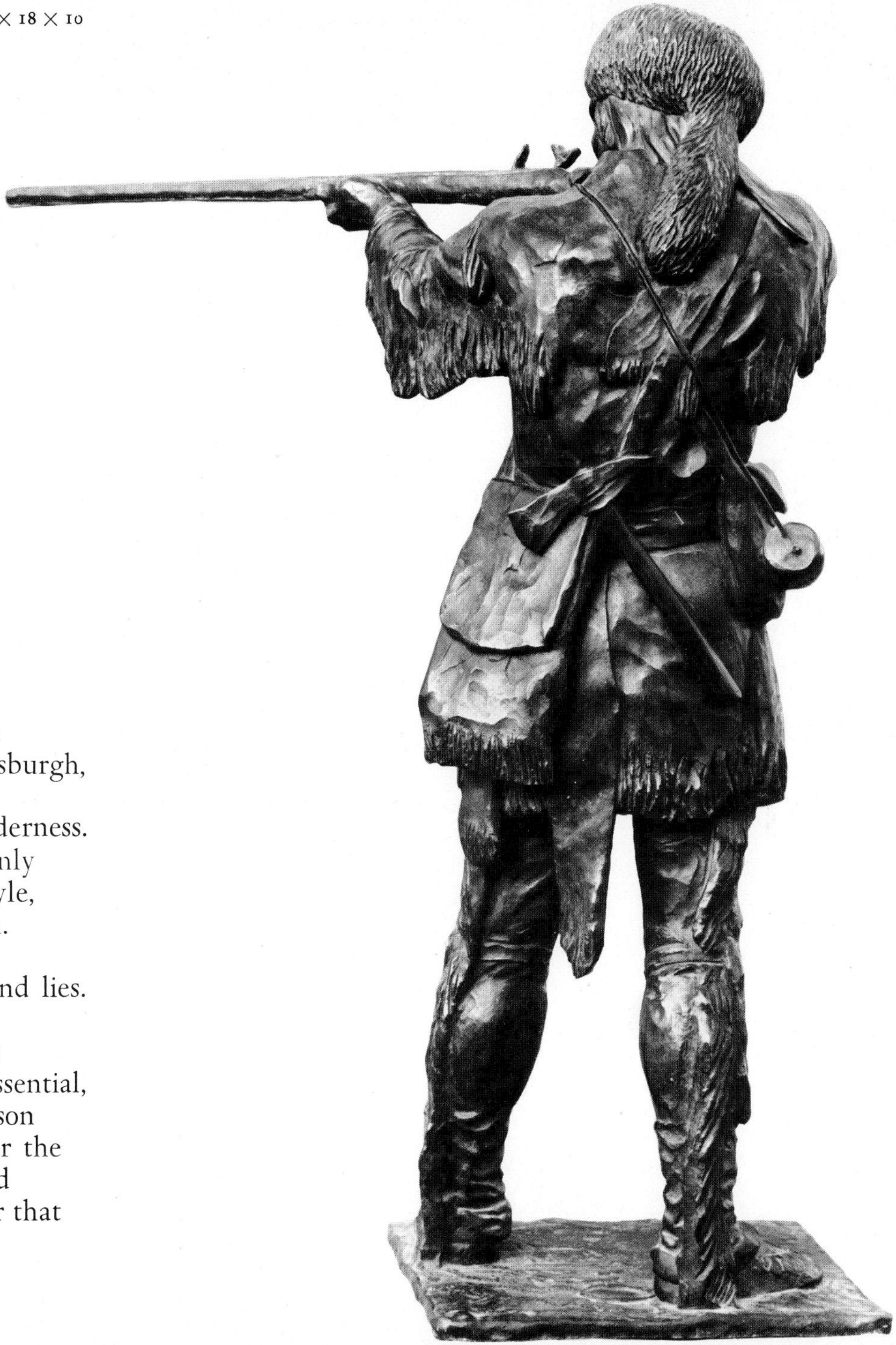

Before the frontiersman made his way into Western Pennsylvania, came the trapper up from Virginia, which claimed a royal grant that extended northwest past Pittsburgh, across Ohio and beyond.

The Beaver Trapper on page 22 slopes through the wilderness. Like the Indian, from whom he learned so much, not only of his specific trade, but, more important, of his life style, the Trapper seems to bend with the bend of the terrain. The Frontiersman takes a stand and shoots it out. The Trapper accommodates himself to the way the land lies. The accommodation is in every muscle of the lithe, balanced figure with the easy, steady stride. The rifle is simply there, handy, to be used if needed. But it is not essential, as it is for both the Frontiersman and the Indian. His reason for being is in the pack of raw beaver hides slung over the shoulder. These prized skins would soon enter into world commerce and, in their humble way, set off a world war that would settle the destiny of the continent. Shown here,

along with the earliest rough drawings, is the as yet incomplete
original wax of the *Trapper* figure, the starting point
in the involved process from which permanent, lasting
bronze emerges. The beauty of wax is its complete receptiveness:
it takes whatever the artist gives and
transmits his marks to metal.

In Harry Jackson's method, the original wax is not the lost wax.
The original, solid figure, is used to make a rubber-based
mold. Into that hollow mold is poured liquid wax to
form a thin coating on both halves. That wax is filled
with and immersed in liquid fire clay which forms the " core "
and the surrounding " investments " or protective outer
shell for the fragile wax. Baking in a furnace hardens
the fire clay but melts the thin reproductory wax which
runs off and goes up in smoke; hence the name " lost wax. "
Air is now where the wax was, while the inner core and
the outer investment of fire clay are kept apart by pins.
Into the air space is poured the bronze, with due allowance
made for the escape of heated air and gases. When, after 24 hours,
the cooled mold is broken open, the bronze is hardened
into the space of the empty air, which had been the space
of the melted wax, which had coated the rubber mold,
which had conformed to the original, solid wax sculpture.
The whole process, at least 5,000 years old, is a cross between
the house that Jack built and looking into a mirror that faces
another mirror.

The fourth central Pitt Mural figure to be made into
bronze is the Indian chieftain from the French alliance.
Even as the Frontiersman and the Trapper take their way of
life from the Indian, so here, the Indian is seen crossing
his way with the European. The musket is the immediate
clue to this change. Like whiskey and the horse,
firearms came from the European coast to the Indian interior.
But that firm stance of resistance, so like the Frontiersman's,
is the real point of contact and omen for the future of the West.

**The " Trapper " and the " Algonquin Chief, " opposite page, still
unfinished waxes, together with these drawn studies, help greatly
in defining their counterparts in the final mural.**

BEAVER TRAPPER, UNFINISHED STATE 19³/₄ × 14¹/₂ × 7

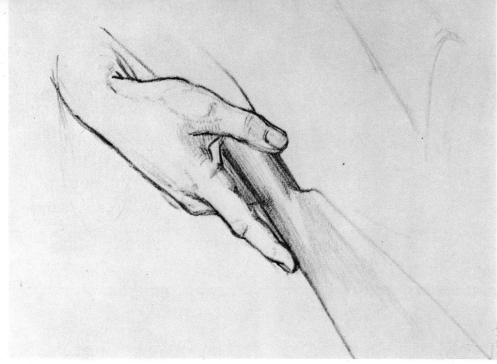

Hand on musket muzzle, drawing $13^{1}/_{4} \times 14^{1}/_{2}$

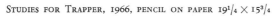

Studies for Trapper, 1966, pencil on paper $19^{1}/_{4} \times 15^{3}/_{4}$

Algonguin Chief, unfinished state $21 \times 14 \times 12$

Europe and Figurative Painting

The painting, opposite, done in 1956, represented for many artists and critics Jackson's tragic abandonment of abstract art and, even worse, treason to " the movement " and to the only legitimate way to paint at mid-century.
With this painting Jackson abandoned the galling limits of abstraction, a considerable personal achievement, and it was his first major translation of the masters into his own work.
Choice of subject was simple: he painted some friends in New York's " Little Italy. "
After false starts on the West Coast, Jackson arrived in New York in 1946. In 1950 he helped found the second generation of " the movement. " They met at Tony Smith's and Motherwells' Studio 35 to debate a new theory of painting. Jackson's studio was at Broome and Mulberry, over the Mare Chiaro Bar. That's the painting, with the boss, Chris Tenneriello, standing at the left. The artist recalls, " I supplied the wine, Chris loaned the tables, and my friends came upstairs to pose. " The painting, owned by Martha Jackson (no relation), a leading New York dealer in avant-garde art, was immensely important to the painter because " it related directly to life, to a human culture. " *Life* published a nine page essay on Harry Jackson, using this painting to set the theme.
" I like my friends and our culture; how we work, ride, love, play, fight and face death, or how we just sit and take it easy. Anonymous courage and silent

←THE ITALIAN BAR, 1956, OIL ON CANVAS 7 × 9 FEET COLL. MARTHA JACKSON, N. Y. LOANED TO THE MARECHIARO RESTAURANT, N. Y.

Prolonged exposure to the art of Europe's museums from 1954 was a major factor in Jackson's advance from abstraction to figurative art. He constantly instructs himself in composition by drawing after such masters as Rubens (top) and Goya (bottom).

PENCIL DRAWING, 1966 10 × 13 COLL. OF THE ARTIST

PENCIL DRAWING, 1965 9¹/₂ × 10¹/₂ COLL. OF THE ARTIST

Odysseys are all around us — why
dwell on hopelessness and
decay — when the flood came Noah
built a boat, he got drunk later. I see
Noah everywhere, building boats,
drinking — this is what
I want to tell straight and
without sentimentality."
This instinct to celebrate man and his
culture brought Jackson back to the
West as subject for most of his work,
the West that remains his most
important touchstone. This life-size
bronze of Sor Capanna has the same
feeling of a folk culture and a
folk hero adding, with every chord
of music, to its texture.
The late singer was an institution
in the oldest quarter of Rome, and
Jackson the American felt honored
to be commissioned to portray him.
In a way, despite Jackson's brilliant brief
career as a New York abstractionist,
those years are now clearly a
detour on a route in art running
straight from the boyhood
drawings of stockyard people to the
West that dominates his thought
and art. The real reason for
his enlisting in the Marines was
his hope — eventually fulfilled — of
becoming a "Combat Artist."
Again, even while he was at the
center of the avant-garde in New York
painting, a close friend of Pollock,
De Kooning, Kline, David Smith and
Ken Noland, he supported himself as a
scene painter — and learned a lot of
traditional painting.

Sor Capanna, 1962, bronze, 6 feet

The " Sor Capanna " bronze, above, was
installed in piazza dei Mercanti, Rome,
in 1968. The first sculptural study
for this monument is at the left.
On the opposite page
is a life-size painting of an Italian
bagpipe player. At Christmas and Easter these
folk musicians from the wild Abruzzi
mountains in the High Appennines descend
to the towns and villages and play
traditional airs.
This one posed for Jackson in 1957.

"You find the last vestiges there of the Renaissance studios. They were mostly foreigners yet they all spoke the same language with the brush. I learned painter's geometry, how to imitate marble and wood, but more important, I learned how to cover large surfaces."

Despite early critical success as an abstract painter, he began then to copy Old Masters at the Metropolitan and other museums, to the increasing dismay of his friends. Yet these years of abstraction were not wasted because when practiced seriously, it forces the painter back to the essential qualities of painting; i.e., composition and the true relations of line, form and color, in a stark way that figurative painting can too easily evade by hiding behind the subject matter. In his impassioned

SKETCH, INK ON PAPER 1957 6¹/₂ × 9

SKETCH, INK ON PAPER 1957 5¹/₂ × 9

ITALIAN BAG PIPER, 1957, OIL ON CANVAS 36 × 72 →

THE PLAINSMAN, 1961, BRONZE 10 × 8 × 7   STUDY, PITT MURAL, 1967, CHARCOAL ON PAPER 14½ × 22   FRANK, 1963, OIL ON CANVAS COLL. OF DR. A. ZORGNIOTTI, N. Y.

In these characteristically perceptive portraits (above) each from a different world — a Wyoming plainsman called Bert, Werner the Swiss painter, and Frank the caretaker of the artist's New York studio — Jackson unerringly reveals the universally human spirit essential to all such men, even while he rejoices in their strong individuality and uniqueness.

experience of the art of the museums and in conversations with Thomas Hart Benton — Pollock's teacher and the towering master of American art in the thirties, also a Western painter — Jackson's realization that all principles of abstraction were already comprehended and practiced by the Old Masters, was confirmed. Thus his figurative painting was profoundly enriched by his abstract period. A purely human value Harry Jackson

found in his years as an abstract painter was, however, that sense of community he has always sought, and found in the West, in the Marines and with stage set painters. The New York avant-garde of the late 1940's and early 1950's was unappreciated by the art public at large. The avant-garde was far from the chichi, high-priced commodity it is now. It was a community of passionately dedicated people, intently pursuing

GIULIA LORIMER, 1958, OIL ON CANVAS, 16 × 20
COLL. OF MR. AND MRS. GEORGE LORIMER, FLORENCE

SARAH JACKSON, 1966, BRONZE 21 × 16 × 10
COLL. OF THE ARTIST

their private dreams of art.
Jackson could not linger long in this
specialized world, but he kept
its austere aesthetics and his feeling
for its artists.
Both the full length portrait of
Robert Lax, the poet, and the portrait
of Mrs. George Lorimer reveal that
humanity in their introspective
concentration, reminiscent of El Greco.
Done a decade later, the bust of the
artist's wife, Sarah, shows that
same concern.

In 1951, while riding after cattle
with his old friend Cal Todd, Jackson
fell into a spirited description of
Wyoming's beauty and the fascination
that cowboy life held for him.
"Harry," said Todd, "we see things
alike. I wish you would
paint about something we both
understand."
Jackson knew then that
"I want to paint
the people, horses and
situations that excite and please me."

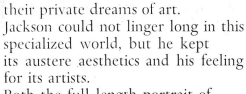

←THE POET, ROBERT LAX, 1962, OIL ON CANVAS 35 × 68½

29

Stampede

Finding his way around among the great painters of Europe, Jackson in the mid-1950's had discovered and been smitten by Courbet's great *Burial at Ornans*. At about the same time he had a conversation with his friend and fellow Wyomingite, Robert Coe, the American ambassador to Denmark. Coe wanted a pair of epic paintings about the American Cowboy for the Whitney Museum of Western Art in Cody. The museum was named for Gertrude Vanderbilt Whitney, who also founded the Whitney Museum in New York, but the Coe family has been equally generous to the institution. Robert Coe is also an amateur painter of competence. In the Louvre, standing before the *Burial at Ornans*, Jackson recounted his dream of painting a cowboy burial set in the vast cattle country that Coe and he knew so well. The heroic mural size painting *Range Burial* was commissioned by the Coe Foundation as a result of this conversation, as was its logical companion piece, *Stampede*. The youth being laid to earth in the *Burial* met his death beneath the stampeding herd, a common enough event in the West. Stampedes, sudden courageous death and lonely unmarked graves form the central

STAMPEDE STUDY, 1964, OIL ON CANVAS 19 × 40

STAMPEDE STUDY, 1964, OIL ON CANVAS 19 × 40

These early studies for "Stampede" above and below block in the central drama in terms of large tonal masses.

themes of the cowboys' saga.
This timeless epic comes to us in every
song and ballad and tale of a
formidable oral tradition, alive
even now in the remote reaches
of the cow-country.
Jackson still sings the songs that
passed the time when, before the war,
he lived in the cowcamps or with
the Burkes and Deckers.
He never learned to play an
instrument. "Hardly anyone
played the guitar," he said,
"outside Helen Hillbury
who cooked at Rose Creek when
my leg was busted once; we sang
all the time. Lee Wentworth could
play anything that wouldn't play
him back, and still can. Hugh Maller
can sing and play as pretty as he
can ride and rope.
I believe old Hugh could strum
a lullabye on a wildcat's whiskers
and make the kitty hum the
harmony." Instinctively Jackson sensed
that through these ballads the
cowboy had distilled his ideal for a
code of life. They tell of his courage
and the pride in his cow-sense
and his ability to ride "anything
that grows hair;" his silent and
boastful side, his loyalty in the face
of danger and his bone deep
independence, the reflections of
habitually lonely men a long way
from women, the timeless natural
wisdom coupled to picture-postcard
sentimentality that danger-filled
loneliness always breeds.

STAMPEDE STUDY, 1964, EGG TEMPERA ON PANEL 22 × 48

STAMPEDE STUDY, 1964, EGG TEMPERA ON PANEL 22 × 48 COLL. DR. & MRS. PAUL ESSERMAN, N. Y.

The two later studies on this page attempt to bring the mass and the details together in a surging sea of cattle beneath the deluge.

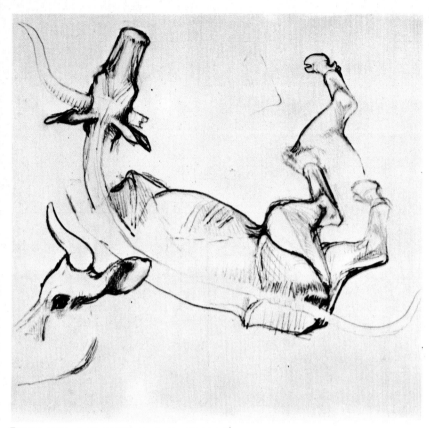

FALLEN STEER, 1964, PENCIL ON PAPER 9¹/₂ × 10³/₄

Drawing, above, and bronze, at right, illustrate Jackson's use of sculpture as a study for a painting. In the mural and in the bronze, the steer has fallen into the muddy draw where a saddle-horse is dragging its condemned rider. In translating the drawing into sculpture, the artist achieves the actual mass with its invaluable lights and shadows. The broken horn emphasizes the little tragedy within the immense action.

For Jackson these songs contain the living spirit that pervades his sculpture and painting and fills them with unique vitality.

In 1959 he recorded 30 of them for a Folkways Album entitled "Harry Jackson, The Cowboy, His Songs, Ballads and Brag Talk" which has become an important collector's item in its own right.

One of the most important qualities of Harry Jackson's work arises directly from his youth in Wyoming and his realization that being a cowboy is not only a job but a way of life. His cowboys are real people, not actors, and not heroes — except when the work demands it.

One job that calls for heroism is a stampede — ninety years ago great herds trailed north and cowboys still sing of stampedes and death, which were all just part of a day's work.

Perhaps no animal appears more placid than a cow, but their half wild longhorn antecedents could be mean critters

STAMPEDE, DETAIL OF FALLEN STEER

Stampede, final study, 1965, egg tempera and oil on panel 22 × 48

with twitching skin and flicking tails. They were quick to panic and once started, hard to stop. A herd of longhorns took on a kind of oversoul, like a maddened human mob — it spelled trouble for the cowboy. The herd, once out of his control, could scatter to hell and never would all be regathered. It would have lost tons of meat, the accumulation of capital and patient labor. A stampede is costly. It is also dangerous. Because of their intrinsic code of loyalty, the cowboys ride to halt it, either by holding them together until the leaders stop, or by turning the herd into a milling ever-tightening circle. This requires hard riding, cow sense, exquisite timing, cast iron guts — and luck.

This small painting mysteriously becomes as big as " all out doors. " It is the last definitive study for the final 21-foot painting and successfully draws all the diversified previous studies and sculpture into a single awesome statement as preparation for the mural on pages 35-36.

33

Jackson's *Stampede* painting centers on one cowboy whose luck has run out. Fallen from his saddle-horse with one foot caught fast in the stirrup, his dragging weight throws the horse head-first into a muddy death-filled draw. The bad luck of being "hung up" in the stirrup was not the only thing that killed him, for he was bound to have been trampled to death even had he fallen free. But it prolonged his last moments and we see him starkly realizing what has happened; the certainty of death in the stiff arms and rigid fingers over his head strike the same apocalyptic note of agony and loss as those of the executed man in Goya's *The 3rd of May*.

The young cowboy's death is the central act in the painting much more than in the sculpture. It is he who is mourned in the companion work, *Range Burial*. Yet, despite the brilliant shaft of light that falls on that central action, it takes its place within an extensive and expertly plotted and painted panorama. The line storm that caused the stampede comes down like the deluge in the Bible, massive, thunderous and unrelenting, fascinating in its wide range of colors and lights. Beneath that scourge from heaven, the herd stretches like the waves of the sea to infinity. In the foreground, horned heads, one with a "death like" black and white marking, stand out from the surge of bone and muscle. Only one of the cowboys, aware of the youth's fall, futilely attempts to "turn" the nearest steers by reining his mount straight onto them, but his hopeless attempt only plays up the inevitability of the fallen rider's death.

Old cowboy ballads tell endlessly of death in stampedes as in these two verses from the classic "Little Joe the Wrangler:"

Twixt the streaks of lightnin' we could see the horse there out ahead | 'Twas Little Joe the Wrangler in the lead, | he was ridin' ol' Blue Rocket, his slicker fer a blind, | trying ta turn them lead steers in their speed. | Well we gets 'em kinda millin' and sorta quieted down | and the extra guard back to the camp did go | but one of them is missin' and we all see at a glance |' tis our little lost horse jingler, Wrangler Joe.

The prime difference between the painting on this page and the sculpture on the overleaf is that in the mural, the whole, vast action is contained within the even vaster expanse of land and sky and wild weather. In the bronze, there are many, many fewer steers, one less cowboy, and the powerful, rhythmic action is contained within itself, a complex but essentially single action with fewer, more clearly defined parts. "Stampede" was one of two murals, the second being "Range Burial" (page 52), commissioned by the William R. Coe Foundation for the Gertrude Vanderbilt Whitney Museum of Western Art in Cody, Wyoming. This work, which is ten feet high and twenty-one feet long, has been shown at the National Cowboy Hall of Fame, Oklahoma City, Oklahoma, and at the Amon Carter Museum, Fort Worth, Texas.

STAMPEDE, 1960/66, OIL ON CANVAS 10 × 21 FEET COLL. WHITNEY GALLERY OF WESTERN ART, CODY, WYO.

What the bronze necessarily loses in the sheer sweep of the
open country and big sky, it more than makes up for
in the masterful articulation of the masses.
Isolated from the broad country that contains
it in the painting, the bronze herd is made to work
together like the instruments of an orchestra,
responding one to another, making smaller
movements and variations on them, all coming together
in a rolling, undulating, powerful surge like that of a
Beethoven symphony. Jackson's intense study of the
Old Masters stands him in good stead: *Stampede* is a Baroque
masterpiece that Bernini or Giambologna — had they
known about cowboys and cattle — would not have been
ashamed of.
The fallen youth, in the absence of the light in the painting,
is set out from the mass, "framed" by the underside
of his own horse, the pointing horns of the steer above his
elbow, two details not in the painting at all, by his hat,
the lariat on his saddle, and finally by the ground itself,
here raised as if it were a platform, the opposite of the
grave the body will occupy in *Range Burial*.
The theme of the bronze is set by the two steers rounding
the lower right of the piece as seen on the fold-out page.
Their breaking out of the mass is a note echoed all the way
over on the lower left, as one lone steer breaks out
and seems, at the same time, to be drawing back from
that isolation.
The cowboy on the right, although distracted momentarily by
the effort not to trample his companion's body, is basically
still attempting to handle the herd, trying to regain
control over its immense force. The front rider, having
fought his way to the fore, races to turn the lead steers,
trying, by pistol fire, to start the herd turning back on itself.
The whole composition builds up to the magnificent
cresting of the lead steers, shown on the following page
in detail. They come on as graceful as dancers and as
certain as death in the ballad "Utah Carroll:" *While leanin' out
of his saddle | atryin' that rope to displace | He falls in front of
them critters | On their mad and deadly race.*

STAMPEDE, STUDY, 1968, RED CHALK ON PAPER 18 × 14

**The fruitful interaction between differing media never
ceases as drawings lead to sculpture which
in turn help produce paintings.
The drawing above and the lithograph (page 34)
were done after both the final
bronze and mural were completed.**

←STAMPEDE, 1958/59, BRONZE 60¹/₄ × 25 × 16

The cowboy culture — and it is a culture — traces a remarkable descent from the Spaniards who brought it to the American Southwest, having, in turn, received the bull mystique from its dim origins in Crete and Assyria at the other end of the Mediterranean. Jackson's bronze head of a steer would be understood and embraced as one of their own by these "cowboys" of antiquity.

LONGHORN STEER, 1968, BRONZE $7 \times 8^1/_2 \times 6^3/_4$

41

"Stampede" is so tightly composed
that the artist extracted from it,
for individual pieces, only the steer's
head and this cowboy,
"Hazin' in the Leaders."

HAZIN' IN THE LEADERS,
1959, BRONZE 12 × 11¹/₄ × 3³/₄

RANGE BURIAL, FINAL STUDY, 1962 19 × 40 COLL. JOHN RYAN, FORT WORTH, TEXAS

Range Burial

The young cowboy killed in "Stampede" is laid to rest.

Harry Jackson has said that *Range Burial* is the product of Courbet's *Burial at Ornans* and dozens of cowboy songs on the theme, the best known undoubtedly being "Bury Me not on the Lone Prairie." The painting has the formal qualities of the Courbet and the humanity of the plaintive harmonica at a campfire. Perhaps the oddest response to the painting, the artist's most ambitious work when he embarked on the long process of creating it, was given by the director of a museum of Western art, of all things, when he said, "Young fellow, John Q. Public will not buy death." It is an easy assumption on the part of people who do not really know the public. Art in general has been about death, probably more than it has been about anything.

As many cowboy songs witness, violent death and Spartan burial are deeply a part of American folk culture, and most markedly so in the cowboy's western domain. Take these few lines, for example:

" *Oh bury me not on the lone praire | these words come soft and mournfully | from the pale lips of a youth who lay | on his bed-tarp at the close of day. | We heeded not his dying prayer | so we rolls him up and plants him there| in a narrow grave just six by three | and his bones now rot 'neath the lone prairie.* " The western tradition of " death dealing cattle " comes to us through Mexico from its origin in the historic bull ritual of the Mediterranean, a ritual extending from the age-old horn-leaping of Crete and bull wrestling of Rome, to the cape work of Madrid.

STUDY OF DEAD MAN, 1962, CHARCOAL ON PAPER

←STUDY OF DEAD MAN, HEAD AND SHOULDERS, 1962, CHARCOAL ON PAPER

The simple stoic cowboy burial descends from Spartan fields in the cradle of Western civilization. The ancient Spartan code and the bull ritual were barely changed in the cowboy way of life from the Tex-Mex country well north into Canada. Jackson's work especially reflects this continuity for he is at home in both these worlds.

In the cities we hide death and hide from it. If we don't see it, it isn't real, despite the violence in the streets around us. In the range country, when death follows the violence of the stampede, the comrades of the fallen man dig a grave and lay him in it. There is no one else to do it, no professionals, no agreed upon ceremony to blur the sharp edge of the final fact of life, the fact of death. The men who rode with the youth beneath the broad sky now give him his home beneath the hard earth.

A cowboy's job has no regular hours and there is little he doesn't do when it needs doing. Horsemen who, in their year, can build fence, doctor sick animals, repair a wagon, build a cabin and dig water holes, can deal with death. It takes a shovel and a pick and, if some is handy,

a length of white linen, or more likely the canvas " tarp " cover of the dead man's bedroll or a threadbare saddle blanket. Death on the range is a lonely thing, as the song says, but it is also another task for the cowboy. He does it with compassion for the dead man, with dispatch and with skill.

The two working cowboys on the opposite page beautifully express the reality of life in the cow country. They're tough, hard-working men, with nothing in the least glamorous about them. But they're genuine and out of their genuineness flows the moment of true mourning for the fallen youth that Harry Jackson has caught in the charcoal sketches.

The artist's method is something like that of certain mid-century movie makers in both Europe and America, or for that matter, some of the greatest directors of the early years of film. He starts with an idea and an overall layout and then begins assembling his characters. The characters, in turn, as they develop reality, inevitably affect and change the original layout, the final arrangement being

Two early small paintings of " Range Burial " reveal the artist as set designer or stage director. The figures remain essentially the same, but the light changes and the horses are moved.

With complete understatement, Jackson, in the sketches on the opposite page, blocks in the moment, of the mourning of the cowboys for their dead companion.

RANGE BURIAL STUDY, 1962, FIRST VERSION, OIL ON CANVAS 19 × 40

RANGE BURIAL STUDY, 1962, SECOND VERSION, OIL ON CANVAS 19 × 40

STUDIES FOR RANGE BURIAL, 1961,
CHARCOAL ON PAPER

RANGE BURIAL STUDY, 1959, EGG TEMPERA ON PANEL 24 × 48

An early realization of the artist in contemplating his Cody mural
commission was that the sense of the limitless sweep of the
range would have to be conveyed. This feeling, so immediate and
awesome in the completed mural is but indicated in the numerous oil,
tempera and ink sketches and, of course, completely absent
from the two bronze versions. In the lithograph on the opposite page,
the painter translated the finished mural into a strongly linear
composition: the figures against the stretch of the land and the
infinity of the sky. The pyramid, the most stable of forms,
provides the inner composition. The head of the mounted man
is the apex. The other two corners are the saddle on the left
and the hats and shovel on the right.

48

arrived at after dozens of such changes in every stage of the process, the rough overall sketches in charcoal or oil or tempera, the individual drawings of people and details are all significantly equal with the painted and patinaed bronzes in his impassioned realization of a final overall vision. Except for foundations, universities and the state and national governments, art patronage is somewhat unfashionable today, both in practice and in conversation. The patron is vaguely felt to be undemocratic or an infringement on the artist's freedom.

Yet the history of art is full of the achievement of what must be called inspired patronage, from Pope Julius's desire to have the ceiling of his chapel painted, to Henry Adams's wish for a fitting memorial to his wife. At a crucial point in his steadily growing career, Harry Jackson was fortunate enough to encounter an inspired patron in Robert Coe and his family Foundation.

This was not merely a matter of the original mural commission for *Range Burial*, although that heroic project lifted Jackson from a routine of doing one work at a time while doing outside work for a living. It gave him a large project within which he could pursue many related ones. It also, and this was very important, showed the artist that someone with knowledge and taste believed in his work. But Coe's patronage went even further. As the painter attempted his large mural, he discovered the problems of scale and of compositions containing many figures. To solve them, he executed, at Pietrasanta, his first two small bronze figures. These he took to Coe. The ambassador purchased them on the spot, and demanded that the artist carry the rough sculptural studies for the two mural canvases to completion and cast the two groups in bronze. From this Jackson came to recognize that he had talent in sculpture and began using it both in relation to the murals and for itself. He returned to the foundry in Italy and began at once to develop the final versions of these complex works directly in wax.

RANGE BURIAL, LITHOGRAPH, EDITION OF 25, 1968 25 × 18

PLANTIN', DETAIL, BRONZE

The inherent dignity and pathos
of the subject are fully conveyed
in the completed mural.
The artist broke the perfect
symmetry of some of the
earlier sketches; but with all the
dry simplicity of the composition,
there is a powerful and complex
geometry at work. The pyramid
bounded by the mounted man, the
shovel and the saddle, is intersected
by two concentric rings: one formed
by the mounted man at the center
and the standing men, all at rest and
contemplating the dead youth,
and within that ring, the
smaller, active ring of three men
working together, wrapping
the youth in a makeshift shroud,
going about their duty with a
kind of gentle efficiency. The entire
group has its base along the raw cut of
the grave. The light falls brightest
on the head and arm of the dead
youth and, most brightly, on our
side of the grave, stopping abruptly
for the darkness of the grave. The land
and the sky go on forever. The new
grave will be a brief landmark in a
country with few. In January 1964 Peter
Hurd wrote: "The *Range Burial* in
my opinion is absolutely superb!
The painting communicates the
poignancy and inevitable awesomeness
of death. The austere landscape with
the infinite plains is a perfect setting
for the burial. The figures are
absolutely convincing as true types,
yet possess a biblical timelessness."

50

"Range Burial" was the companion piece to the "Stampede" commissioned for the Gertrude Vanderbilt Whitney Museum of Western Art in Cody, Wyoming. Before its presentation to the museum, the painting, which is ten feet high and 21 feet long, was exhibited in New York and at the National Collection of Fine Arts of the Smithsonian Institution in Washington. More recently it has hung together with the "Stampede" painting in the National Cowboy Hall of Fame, Oklahoma City, and the Amon Carter Museum, Fort Worth. Cal Todd, the artist's friend of 30 years posed for the man holding his hat by the brim.

THE RANGE BURIAL, 1963, OIL ON CANVAS 10 × 21 FEET COLL. WHITNEY GALLERY OF WESTERN ART, CODY, WYO.

Although the artist got into sculpture in the first place as an aid to painting, this second bronze version of the "Range Burial," called "The Plantin'" is entirely different from the painting, and acknowledges Jackson's grasp of the profound difference between the two forms of art.

The detail, opposite, shows one of the many half wild dogs that lived along the cattle trails scavenging from the chuck wagons. Scared, yet curious, he sniffs out death.

PLANTIN', 1960, BRONZE 13 $\times$ 26^1/$_2$ $\times$ 12^1/$_2$

If *Stampede* in bronze recalls the bravura sculptural performance of the Baroque period, the *Range Burial*, in both versions, harkens back to an earlier period of Italian sculpture, that from the Pisanos to Ghiberti. The scene suggests nothing so much as an early Renaissance favorite subject, *The Deposition*, that moment in the passion of Christ when the body is taken down from the cross before burial.

In the Italian tradition, the body is normally portrayed as lying on the ground, its upper part held by the Mother and surrounded by mourners, both humans and angels.

Harry Jackson has chosen a related sort of moment in the burial sequence for the bronze versions, a moment when the full weight of the body is on the attending mourners. The blasted tree suggests a cross and astonishingly, the mounted man on our right actually recalls a similar figure placed by Rembrandt in the first state of his great etching, *The Three Crosses*, as well as the horseman in the center background of Tintoretto's *Descent from the Cross*.

The inner dynamics of *The Plantin'*, opposite, are not only different from those of the figure group in the painted mural, they are almost the precise reverse. In the painting, the central form is the pyramid, with the apex held by the single mounted man in the center of the outer circle of cowboys.

Here, the horse has been moved away from the center and multiplied by four. There are two mounted men and two riderless horses, one pair to each side. The two standing men are transitions in height from the mounted men and from the blasted tree to the lower level of the three men kneeling to bear the weight of the shrouded body and to the lowest level of all, that of the man standing in the grave to help lower the burden to earth.

Thus the pyramid that, in the painting, took the earth for its base and rose to the mounted man, here is formed by the two mounted men and reaches its reversed apex in the grave itself, below the shoulders of the man in the grave.

Besides suggesting — for students of art history, or for Christians — the cross of Calvary, the blasted tree in the sculpture must do in its limited form what, in the painting, is accomplished by the limitles expanses of sky and plain; namely suggest not only the geographical extent of the locale but also the emotive implications of that geography: the loneliness, the isolation, the need for the self-sufficiency that is seen in almost every cowboy figure by Harry Jackson.

That complex of intangibles is summed up in the bare, dead and split open hulk of a tree, but the tree is only the strongest and most visible element in a whole web of things that subtly make the point.

The lone figure standing almost at attention beside the tree contributes; so do the two riderless horses, which, between them, form the outermost boundaries of the group; the ground itself is so worked in the bronze as to suggest the waves of the infinite and lonely sea.

PLANTIN', DETAIL OF DOG

WHERE THE TRAIL FORKS, DETAIL

Jackson's painted bronzes are never merely reproductions of figures in the paintings or in group sculptures. The painted bronzes serve the artist's purposes in getting the feel of a group, its weight, mass and color relations, and especially its emotional relations. "Where the Trail Forks," the painted bronze above, resembles the drawing at right more closely than either resembles the corresponding figure in the "Range Burial" painting or in the bronze group.

WHERE THE TRAIL FORKS, CHARCOAL STUDY, 1962

CHARCOAL STUDY, 1962

Another drawing, above, catches the face of the final figure, but has different hair and a different disposition of the arms. In drawing and bronze, the body slumps in mourning.

The great strength of Harry Jackson's painted bronzes is that although they were created, many of them, in strict relationship to bronze sculptural groups and to figure groups in large-scale paintings, the individual figures also have a life of their own and stand independently as solitary pieces. In the individual cowboys made in relation to *Range Burial*, that quality of being solitary has another meaning. Each of the figures in both the mural and in the two bronze groups is solitary before the fact of death, and that quality is strongly conveyed in the painted bronzes. This standing cowboy is close to the center of all three groups. The removal of his hat acknowledges the fact of death. It also reveals the little strip of his forehead that, sheltered by the hat brim, has not been burned by the sun, tanned and hardened by hard days. That strip of white flesh is also a sign of the man's vulnerability, of human vulnerability in the face of death. His dangerous calling gives him long lonely periods to reflect on how fragile he and his bravest companions are before nature's forces. The title signifies that this cowboy, standing reflectively at the "Fork," stays on the old trail while his dead partner takes the one "across the Great Divide." Both he and the figure on the following page, named after the ballad, "Cowboy's Meditation," bring its words to life.

WHERE THE TRAIL FORKS, 1962,
PAINTED BRONZE 19^1/$_2$ × 5^3/$_4$ × 5^1/$_2$

57

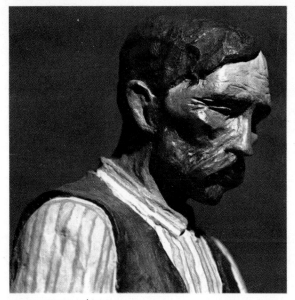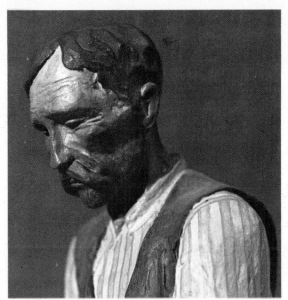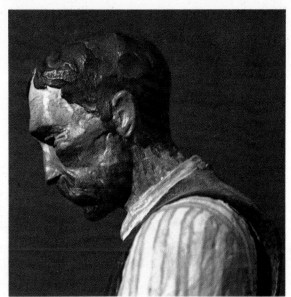

DETAILS OF RIDER'S HEAD

The full-length view, opposite, and the three close-ups, above, show the sensitive interpretation of low-keyed emotions in this figure.

Both horse and rider pause and bow their heads to death on the plain. In the nature of things, and especially in the nature of the cowboy's work, a mounted man is less vulnerable than a man on foot.
For that reason, there is added pathos to the human vulnerability to death expressed in the standing cowboy when it is seen here in the mounted one.
But this mourner is older than the man on foot.
He has seen death more often, in more varied circumstances. He has seen enough of it to be fully convinced of its inevitability. That conviction lies behind the humble nobility of the cowboy's life, as it lends nobility to all trades of constant danger and sudden risks.
Animals catch the mood of those around them and particularly of those with whom they work every day. The horse in this sculpture, with no equine histrionics movingly underlines the feelings of the rider and of the occasion.

Perfectly still, with head bowed and tail conforming to the curve of the flank, the beast repeats, on a broad scale, the sentiment of mourning.
But the horse in this subdued, contained position does something else, too. If the mounted man is less vulnerable than the man on foot, that degree of invulnerability is weakened, lessened, when the mount stills itself and draws in upon itself like this.
Thus the rider as well as the man on foot expresses human vulnerability to death along with his mourning for the dead cowboy.
Because the rider does so from a position that is normally stronger, there is additional pathos.
In painting, the artist has to choose a single angle of view. In his painted bronzes, Jackson studies the entire figure or any detail from all sides. In the three views above of the rider's head and drooped shoulders, the various angles add immeasurably to the impact.

←COWBOY'S MEDITATION, 1964, PAINTED BRONZE 22 × 20 × 9½   59

Harry Jackson thinks the word
"gunsil" is a belittling abbreviation of
"gunslinger" still used out west;
i.e., "He's just a Gunsil," or an
equally local term, "pistol,"
"Ain't but a Pistol kid," to deflate
a swollen-headed youngster.
In criminal slang there is a similar
word, "Gunsel," with the older
meaning and something of the
Western meaning, which
is that of a cocky kid, a little
too big for his britches,
given to throwing about what weight
he has and enthralled with the idea
of himself as a man in a man's world.
When kids like Jackson's *Gunsil*
shoulder a man's job, the bragging
invented to steel their untried
courage is so unprintably wild that
only the following is quoted:
"*I was born full-growed with nine
rows of jaw teeth and holes
bored for more. There was spurs
on my feet and a rawhide quirt in my
hand, and when they opens the
chute I come out ridin' a panther
and a-ropin' the long-horned whales.
I've rode everything with hair on it...
and I've rode a few things that
was too rough to grow hair.
I've rode bull moose on the prod,
she-grizzlies and long bolts of lightnin'.
Mountain lions are my playmates and
when I feels cold and lonesome,
I sleeps in a den of rattlesnakes 'cause
they always makes me nice and warm.
To keep alive I eat stick dynamite and
cactus. The Grand Canyon ain't nothin' but*

GUNSIL, STUDY, 1962, CHARCOAL ON PAPER
COLL. LOGAN ENGLISH, KENTUCKY

The third of the three principal characters abstracted from the "Burial" group as painted bronzes is the young cowboy called by the artist "Gunsil." The face reveals expressive values of painted bronze. The lanky youth who posed is the son of Jackson's boyhood friend and fellow artist, Eugene Powell.

←GUNSIL, 1962, PAINTED BRONZE 20 × 6 × 7

my bean hole. When I gets thirsty
I drink cyanide cut with alkali.
When I go to sleep I pillow my head
on the Big Horn mountains, I lay
my boots in Colorada and
my hat in Montana.
I can stretch my arms clean
out from the Crazy Woman Fork plumb
over to the Upper Grey Bull River.
My bed tarp covers half of Texas and
all of Old Mexico. But there's one
thing for sure and certain, and if you
boys wants to know, I'll tell you that
I'm still a long way short
of being the daddy of 'em all... cause he's
full growed and as any man that
really knows can see — well, boys,
I ain't nothin' but a young'un."

The *Gunsil* provides a third variation on the theme of human vulnerability in the face of death. The cockiness is surely portrayed in the figure. The character does not take off his hat, for instance. Yet the beautifully sensitive painting of the face reveals the sudden, unexpected identification with the dead man who was just a young kid like the Gunsil with many years before him.

GUNSIL, DETAIL

61

COWBOY'S MEDITATION, HEAD STUDY, BRONZE 5³/₄ × 4³/₄

Art and man are always combined, whether in the small head above or in the complex group opposite.

The three figures out of the *Burial* group thus provide a trio of differing and related responses to the central fact of the work, which is death. Whether painted or, as above, patinaed bronze, the individual figures are raised to a high degree of detailed finish primarily for the sake of establishing character and mood. In the bronze groups such fine detail is neither necessary nor desirable. Jackson, for instance, has not painted a full sculpture of either the

Burial or *Stampede*. Furthermore, the individual details will be found, on examination, to be less highly developed than in the single figures, painted or unpainted. The reason for this difference is that the group has something else going for it. Especially, it has the relations between figures and the composition of the whole. To allow those values their full play, the detail is suppressed a little. The figures are less finished, their individual emotions carried more by the arrangements of their postures than by the expressions on their faces. This is certainly true of this first version of the bronze *Range Burial*, commissioned by Robert Coe. The people here are much more spread out than in the tight composition of the other bronze burial. The land itself is more extended, more like that of the mural painting. It arches up a little from the plain. The expanded group of cowboys assisting at the burial is arranged to form a majestic arc, suggesting that of the big sky above the limitless plain. Thus the artist has managed to get into bronze some of the feeling of vastness that is so impressive in the painting. The enlarged composition recalls the Renaissance and Baroque masters Jackson has studied most closely. A complex system of triangles and concentric ovals converges upon that hole in the ground where the dead youth is being laid to rest. The mounted men, the riderless mounts, the standing gravediggers, the men on foot and the

dog all stand in silence about the four men lowering the body into its earth. This subject exemplifies Harry Jackson's grasp of the unique cowboy spirit that has held the world enthralled. With bronze and paint he has given durable form to the deep native wisdom that the cowboy most truly recorded in endless ballads and laments. Jackson's work so clearly reveals the insight in these crude refrains that are his inspiration that the heroic spirit they share with the Bible and classic myths become apparent: " Utah Carroll " *" There lies a grave with neither headstone | neither date nor name | and therein lies my partner | 'neath the clay from which he came. | When we buries his body on the spot where he was slain | he's wrapped up in that blanket he used to save his friend. | Everyman upon the cow range who knows how Utah died | will think on him in silence and speak his name with pride. "*

THE RANGE BURIAL, 1958/59, BRONZE 15 × 43 × 23→

The increased scope of the land is emphasized by an increase in the sense of hardness of that land. The rock outcroppings not only provide a dramatic sculptural system of levels for the different characters to rest on; they also convey the hardness of the earth by these unrelenting men and their dead companion they now entrust to that earth.
" I've seen the ' Range Burial ' and the ' Stampede ' at the Amon Carter, and I was very much impressed. These bronzes have sort of knocked me off my feet. They are the real thing. " Thomas Hart Benton

The suggestion of the cross made by the blasted tree above the dead cowboy is furthered by the arrangement of the central group. The grave digger with his shovel provides the vertical axis. The body itself provides the horizontal.

"We wrapped him up in his blanket / And lowered him down in the ground / And covered him over with the boulder stones / Of granite so gray and round."
(Traditional ballad)

RANGE BURIAL, DETAIL

The raw youth of the mourning group from "Range Burial" and "The Plantin'" conveys the same complex emotions in patinaed as in painted bronze.

GUNSIL, 1962, BRONZE 20 × 6 × 7

GUNSIL, DETAIL, BRONZE

The older men, too, in the simplicity of the patinaed bronze, express individually the profound grief that makes this a classic achievement of Western art.

WHERE THE TRAIL FORKS, 1965, BRONZE 19½ × 5¾ × 5½

COWBOY'S MEDITATION, 1964, BRONZE 22 × 20 × 9¾

FLY TIME, SECOND VERSION, 1969, BRONZE 9¹/₂ × 9¹/₄ × 8

Men and Horses

" For my money, and I'm willing to spend a little of it for what should bring a lot more — Harry Jackson has the right words and the right tune both. I'm sure his work is the best of its kind in the country."

J. Frank Dobie

Self-educated, Harry Jackson has evolved some provocative ideas about history as it relates to or is illuminated by his own passion of the West. His central idea, historically, is that the American cowboy represents a rare, perhaps unique, combination of two ways of life most often in bitter conflict: those of the gentleman or knight on horseback and the ordinary workingman. In the history of China, or the Middle Ages, or the Renaissance or the Napoleonic Era, he points out, the agricultural worker was regularly despoiled by the man on a horse. The man on a horse, for his part, had a certain nobility, a code of honor, a spirit of noblesse oblige, which enhanced life for those who professed or encountered it. The American cowboy, almost alone among the historical occupations, combines the mounted nobility — the chivalry — and the ordinary anonimity of the skilled country workingman.

TRAIL BOSS, 1958, BRONZE 8¼ × 8 × 3¼

TRAIL BOSS, DETAIL

The two contradictions are fully coexistent
in "The Trail Boss" above, Jackson's first bronze.
Horse and rider both display an aristocratic grace,
yet both are tough, hardened workers.
"Fly Time," opposite, was cast when Mrs.
H.H. Brittingham, a Fort Worth friend,
saw it in the "Burial"
and commissioned it as a separate work.
Later Jim Griffin of Boise noted the rider
was hatless. Little by little the works change.

The aristocratic display of knightly excellence was never better portrayed than in " The Bronc Stomper," an expert working against an ornery bronc, whose several brands show how often he's been traded off. A perfectly three-dimensional sculpture, the piece reveals a new moment in every angle. The Stomper swears as his rawhide quirt whips the bronc at every jump; but while he tries to spur the horse in the shoulder as well, the saddle bow has slipped under his left leg and may pry him from his perch in a flash. " I feel like I'm ridin' the hurricane deck / of a cyclone and tornado a havin' a wreck ". (Strawberry Roan)

BRONC STOMPER, 1959, BRONZE 17 × 13¹/₂ × 5¹/₂ AND DETAILS

Harry Jackson got into bronze sculpture in the first place as an aid to seeing the figures in large scale mural paintings. In this, as he was aware, he had ample and honorable precedent in the history of art. Tintoretto built miniature stage sets to study the lighting as well as the forms.

Raphael's teacher, Perugino, had the sculptor Sansovino make for him a group of wax figures to use as a model for a *Deposition*. The sculptural group is in the Victoria and Albert Museum, London. In the Prado are the painted sculptures of Adam and Eve made by El Greco.

It took Jackson eight years to complete the murals of *Range Burial* and *Stampede*. At the end of that time, as he said: "I was certain that sculpture had taken an equal place in my heart alongside of painting and that the two were destined to complement and aid each other in the most provocative and as yet undreamt-of ways."

The working quality of the cowboy is summed up in " Center Fire," left, and " Ground Roper," opposite, range hands doing their job. The title of the mounted figure originates from a saddle with a single, center cinch, but it applies to a particular region and cowboy style. This area covers old Mexico and the three Pacific coast states as well as considerable adjoining areas. It's called " Center-Fire Country " in cowboy lingo.

GROUND ROPER, 1958, BRONZE 10 × 5 × 4

GROUND ROPER, DETAIL

Dancers and Musicians

In using sculpture related to painting, Jackson had one precedent more important than the masters of the past. This was the American old master, Thomas Hart Benton, the towering figure of American Regionalist Painting in the 1920's and '30's and the man most responsible for the final liberation of American art from its long European bondage. Jackson never formally studied under Benton, but he has known such affection for him and such strong admiration for his work that he feels like a former student.

DANCERS AND HORSEMAN, OIL ON PANEL 7 × 9 COLL. OF MRS. WILLIAM MEEK, IRELAND

The younger man met the older at the continued insistence of their close mutual friend, Jackson Pollock, who in his turn became the towering figure of abstract expressionists. In 1961 Jackson finally met Benton and saw his Truman Library mural at Independence. This mural further confirmed the younger artist's long held vision of creating heroic, Realist work based upon the American experience. Benton made models for his paintings in plastelline, painted them in full color and moved them about to crystallize the composition.

Jackson began using sculptured models years before they met but had never tried to color them as Benton did. When Benton came to Jackson's Camaiore studio-foundry for a long working stay in 1965 he made and colored a typical figure group as a model for a painting to show the younger man his procedure — an invaluable and sadly too rare form of artistic sharing that has meant a lot to Jackson as a man as well as an artist.

Jackson often is asked whether he is a painter who sculpts or a sculptor who paints. One, his friend Jacques Lipchitz, who helped found twentieth century art, feels that an artist cannot be both. Because Jackson, like Benton, Remington and Degas began sculpting to strengthen the sense of form in his painting, he, like they, will always remain a painter who sculpts. Yet these two media, apparently so different, come together in his studio and influence each other so greatly that they become inseparable. The hight-relief bronze, opposite, shows in fact a remarkably painterly quality. The figures dancing in the glade, the piper, the trees and the ground, even the moon, could have been made in paint, the material flows as from a brush.

Romantic oil sketch left and bronze high-relief opposite show the artist dealing with a timelessly classic motif, but the sense of form and the vivid living touch that bring his horses and cowboys to life are the same.

DANCERS IN A GLADE, 1961, BRONZE HIGH-RELIEF 15¹/₄ × 12³/₄

PIPER, 1964, BRONZE 11 × 8 × 8

MEXICAN DANCER, 1964, BRONZE 14½ × 7½ × 8½

**Figures for a ballet reveal a stark storyline: the piper, the dancer and the beat of the dance set by death.
The feeling for motions is equally present in these dancers and the bronc rider on the following page.**

MEXICAN DEATH DANCER, 1960 BRONZE 15½ × 6 × 4½ AND DETAIL→

↑ SETTIN' PERTY, 1959, BRONZE 16 × 10¹/₄ × 6→

"There ner was a horse / That couldn't
be rode / and there ner was a man /
that couldn't be throwed." The buckin'
bronc and the buster make this an
ideal example of Jackson's mastery of
violent motion.

A similar power appears in this pair of "Peasant Dancers," all music and movement.

PEASANT DANCERS, 1961, BRONZE 11 × 5³/₄ × 6³/₄→

The man and the horse on the opposite page and the man and the woman on this page have more common characteristics than obvious differences. In both groups, there is grace achieved in motion. In both groups, great strength is being exerted, as in the powerful play of muscles in the male dancer's back and arms. In both groups there is an overall effort toward total coordination of the rapid movements of two beings. This kind of revelation of points of contact between persons or millieux superficially very different is one of the rewards of studying the work of Harry Jackson. Even when an artist's obsession with a subject is as deep as Jackson's about the West, the inner subject, which in these two works actually expresses the grace of rhythmic dynamic action, is the deeper emotion. *"His backbone's like a mountain, his legs stiff as poles, | When he hits the ground, boys, he leaves ten foot holes. | It's right at the top of each stiff-legged buck | that he sucks himself back and you're ridin' on luck. | He shoots right straight up and he don't turn around | like he's done give up life way down there on the ground."* (Strawberry Roan)

STEER ROPER, 1959, BRONZE 12 × 25 × 12

The " Steer Roper " pits the live weight of a full grown steer against the teamwork of a top horse and rider. Here one can see how Jackson's abstract and realist abilities happily reinforce one another. The pure force generated by holding two straining masses together with a single taut wire, that would delight Moore or Giacometti, adds an indefinable sense of power and hypnotic balance to this excellently modeled bronze.

TO THE GODS, 1961, BRONZE 22³/₄ × 14 × 5¹/₂

The *Salty Dog* — rangeland dialect meaning a top hand —
seen in three views on the opposite page,
is the quintessential Harry Jackson cowboy, tough, skeptical,
knowledgeable about his work and his country and
reasonably indifferent to things outside both.
The tools of his trade are with him, his gun and his
rope at hand, his spurs on his boots.
He is ready to go and he takes no nonsense.
Coolly he surveys whatever is before him and prepares
to deal with it. He and men like him built the West
and continue to maintain a very large part of it.
" *Had him a head like a hatchet, a face made to
match it | a nose a pelican's beak. |
His legs was all bowed and he was pigeon toed, |
with a chin that was plumb mild and meek. |
Well, he lived in the weather, his hide was like leather,
His hands was all horny and rough, | you could tell
by his stride he was just made to ride, | and no critter for
him was too tough.* " (Iron Pants Pete)
But there was another West before ever the white
man came up from Mexico and over the plains from the
young Republic along the ocean shore.
The Indian's West is long gone, penned up on reservations
and dying for lack of scope.
The easy, natural communication with the Great
Spirit of the Indians characterizes the religious feeling
of the American cowboy much more nearly than
either the elaborate ritual of the Spaniard or the worried
bookkeeping of Eastern Puritanism.
Jackson's mounted Indian expresses that direct address to
the Spirit even as it speaks poignantly of the decline of
the Indian culture itself. Cowboys and Indians fought
each other savagely but both survive as part of the Western
make-up in the world of Harry Jackson.

**In both the rough, unfinished figure of the mounted Indian,
" To the Gods," and the finely detailed bronze, " Salty Dog," Jackson
symbolizes the living spirit of the American West.**

SALTY DOG, 1959, BRONZE 10 × 5 × 4

In an odd way, both these early paintings have in them emotional elements that later went into the conception of the *Range Burial* and the individual sculptures related to that mural. Bobby Dylan had arrived in the Greenwich Village community of artists just as Jackson was leaving, but their paths crossed and the painter from Wyoming could recognize in Dylan's laments the lonely cry of the American cowboy in song, rising above the banality of his lyrics to the flashes of pure poetry that illumine all the original Western music. A genuine expression of this spirit is the small oil *Looking Things Over*. This title covers anything from a man's seriously checking grass, water and stock, to just loafing.

Jackson and Pilcher, a long-time friend and a top working cowboy and rodeo hand, were gathering cattle recently when they stopped to rest the horses. The artist saw the typical way he hunched over, elbows on the saddle-horn, the reins hanging slack, was impressed by the pose, and painted it that evening.

BOBBY DYLAN, THE LONESOME BLUES, 1962.
TEMPERA ON CANVAS 54 × 81

It would be hard to imagine two settings more removed from each other than those of singer Bobby Dylan's squealing young fans and the lone prairie, but Jackson's two paintings bring them together.

LOOKING THINGS OVER, 1964, OIL SKETCH ON PANEL 12 × 16

Lone Hand, detail

The great Westerner, J. Frank Dobie, wrote, "Everyday, nearly, I look at 'The Lone Hand.' Nobody ever made a better back-sag than you've made. He is my people. The whole thing is life to me." This mounted hand embodies the loneliness of a hundred songs that the guitar plucking cowboy sings. His silence and the music are equally eloquent.

←Lone Hand, 1961, bronze 15 × 15 × 6

Perhaps only an outsider can appreciate, and celebrate, a rural community like the West. The finest celebrations of life in the country, from Horace to Beethoven, from Tolstoy to Russell, have been made by city people who were inspired by what the natives took for granted. If so, Harry Jackson is well qualified. Born in the most American of cities, Chicago, Jackson went West in adolescence and knew he was home. He left for war and for art, moving across the globe to Pacific Islands of death, to Manhattan Island and to the ancient peninsula of Italy. But Pitchfork, Wyoming, remains his home. He returns there every year as a bird flies home. From the West he takes most of his subjects, but more important, from there he takes his spirit. Harry Jackson is as ambitious as Cézanne, who announced boldly that he wanted to " re-do Poussin after nature." Jackson as boldly wants to "re-do Europe's museums after the American West." To him these daring, raw-boned people molding a vast wilderness are made of the same epic stuff as the Bible and the Greek Myths.

LONG BALLAD, DETAIL   LONG BALLAD, 1959, BRONZE 6 × 5 × 4→

THE FIRST SADDLE, DETAIL

THE FIRST SADDLE, 1961, BRONZE 12½ × 11 × 9

Bronze of the " First Saddle " placed on a colt catches the cowboy's slow, gentle, practiced firmness, the horse's coiled, trembling, spring-steel fear.

Ropin', 1959, bronze $13^1/_2 \times 17^1/_2 \times 5^1/_4$

With no heroics, a " saddle-hand ", on his loping horse, with his loop spread overhead, tends to his business of " Ropin' " on the lonely range.

STUDY OF HORSES, 1964, PENCIL ON PAPER 9 × 12

STUDY OF HORSES, 1964, PENCIL AND WASH ON PAPER 9³/₄ × 12¹/₂

In Italy Harry Jackson discovered Italian bronze workmanship and made it work for him. But to Italy he has brought more than a touch of the American West. His house in Camaiore is a kind of miniature "Western spread." There is always one horse in residence — his own — and often as many as three, the others left there by itinerant Italian horse traders. Jackson rides and ropes regularly, keeping in practice for his visits home in Wyoming. Always, of course, he draws the horses in pencil or charcoal, as he draws everything that comes before him.

90

This horseman has the vigour of the "Stampede." It and the following drawings are studies for the Pitt mural.

STUDY, CAVALRYMAN, 1967, INK ON PAPER 11 × 5¾→

Artists have a decisive advantage: they can pick their ancestors, and Jackson's choice is varied and illustrious: Giotto, Masaccio, Tintoretto, Titian, Michelangelo. He admires Rubens, an odd affinity one thinks — Jackson's spare, hard Westerners and Rubens' opulent ladies. " By God," he says, " that was a painter's painter!" Jackson has made drawings after all of them; in his sketches one sees Uccello, the Elgin Marbles, Rembrandt, Poussin, Goya, Roman animal bronzes, Delacroix, Courbet, Stubbs, Cézanne, Donatello, Verrocchio, Degas, Baryé and Rodin. The challenge of these great men gives him constant hope of realizing as lasting a work as theirs for his own country and time. These Masters bind him to Europe, but the Americans that draw him back are Bingham, Eakins, Russell, St. Gaudens, Remington, Orozco, Benton and Hurd. Jackson's own country will always be the West. Working in his Tuscan studio, he knows that it and the cowboy on his horse are fit subjects for an art as deep as any that has ever existed. With his vision, abilities and drive, he has already made an impressive start. If it can be done, he's the man to do it.

White Oak, Cooks Forest, Penn.
H.M.J. 8.19.64

WHITE OAK, 1964, PENCIL ON PAPER 13^1/$_2$ × 10

These drawings made in Pennsylvania for the Fort Pitt Mural show Jackson's delight in drawing nature's volumes and textures,

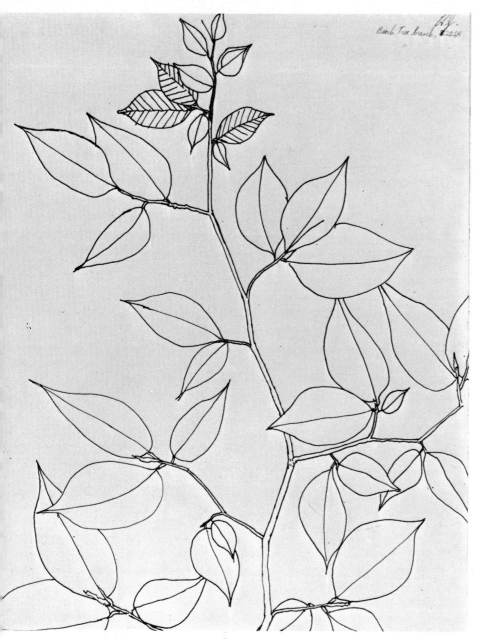

BEECH TREE LEAVES, 1964, PEN ON PAPER 10¹/₂ × 13

. . . . the grace of her flat patterns as a single line describes these leaves

HEMLOCK AND HICKORY, 1964, PENCIL ON PAPER 10 × 13¹/₂

. . . or the combination of texture and pure line above.

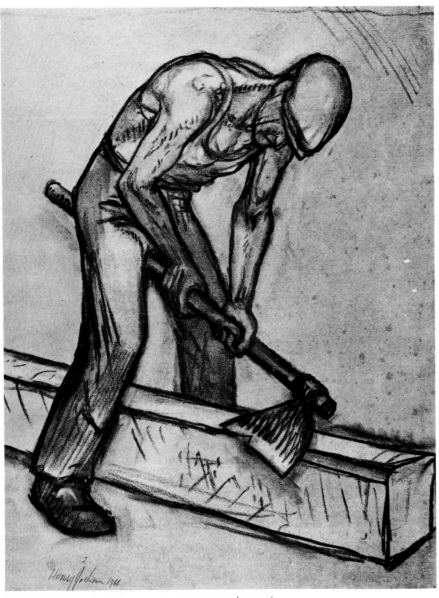

SQUARING A TIMBER, 1966, CHARCOAL ON PAPER 17^1/$_2$ × 23^1/$_2$

An Italian woodsman, squaring chestnut beams for the Jacksons' new house in Camaiore, was used as a model, in part, for a colonial backwoodsman in the settler's panel of the mural.

GRAPE VINE, 1957, INK ON PAPER 7 × 9^1/$_4$

Close observation and sound drawing underline Jackson's art, as in this ink study of a grapevine with tendrils and supporting sticks in field adjoining his place in Italy.

Chronology

1924-31
Born April 18, 1924 in Chicago: only child. Mother, Ellen, deserted by husband, runs lunchroom near Chicago Stockyards. At 5 years begins to ride and draw horses.

1931-38
Scholarship Saturday morning classes, Chicago Art Institute; attends Daniel Catton Rich's lectures on Renaissance art. Constant truant from public school; only interest painting and horses.

1938-42
Runs away to Wyoming; works, Diamond Lumber Co., Cody; Bradford and Frost ranches, Wapiti, and Pitchfork Ranch, Meeteetse, which he regards as home. Befriended and encouraged by the painter Ed Grigware.

1942-45
Joins Marines, landing Tarawa, Roi-Namur, Saipan, twice wounded; at 20 appointed youngest "Official Combat Artist;" accorded first professional exhibitions. CBS chooses Sgt. Jackson as master of ceremonies for "Word from the People" broadcast saluting World Conference, San Francisco, April 1945; introduces prime ministers and great personages including the painter Benton. Narrates film "To the Shores of Iwo Jima," best war documentary Pacific Area; discharged Oct. 1945. Short period as radio actor in Los Angeles, returns to Wyoming.

1946-48
To New York, studies art under Public Law 16 with Tamayo and Hans Hoffmann. Becomes close friend of Jackson Pollock, friends include De Kooning, Kline, David Smith, Dzubas, and Ken Noland.

1949
Marries painter Grace Hartigan, spends year painting in Mexico; brief study with Siqueiros.

1950
Returns to New York; early member of original Artists' Club on 8th Street. Divorced. In first "New Talent" show at Kootz Gallery. Supports self as dishwasher, reinforced concrete worker, joins United Scenic Artists, paints sets for Metropolitan Opera, New York City Ballet, Broadway plays; CBS staff artist. Paints in free time. Meets Jacques Lipchitz in Woodstock, New York; later become close friends in Italy.

1951
In historic "9th Street" group show, in first show at Studio 35 founded by Tony Smith and Motherwell. Paints scenery for summer opera St. Louis, Mo. Takes mother to see his Pitchfork "birthplace" and to meet the Burke/Decker family who adopted him 13 years before in Cody, Wyoming.

1952
First one-man show at Tibor de Nagy Gallery. Jackson is abstract expressionist painter but beginning to change. Begins studying the Old Masters in museums. Long visit to Wyoming. Conversation with old friend Cal Todd has profound effect on the painter's growing desire to paint figuratively.

1953
Second one-man show at Tibor de Nagy, painting more figurative. Assists René Bouché in painting six murals for Packard Co., Detroit. Scene painter, foreman, Rock Creek Summer Opera, Washington, D.C.

1954
Marries Joan Hunt, dancer. Separated 1956, Year's knapsack trip through Europe, copying masterworks and sketching in the great museums.

1955
In New York working again as scene painter and for summer opera Pittsburgh. Critic Clem Greenberg selects painting for Gloria Vanderbilt Purchase Fund.

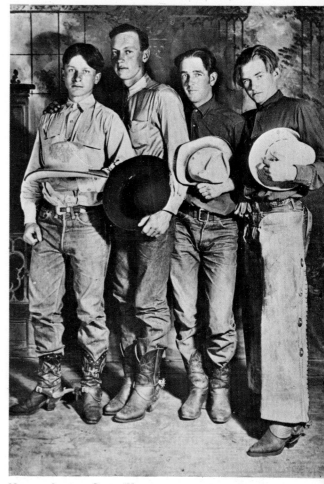

HISCOCK STUDIOS, CODY, WYOMING

The Young Cowboys: Fourth of July 1939. Jackson, 16, on left, with friends Cal Todd, Bill Hendricks and Ken Ellison. The four had left the round-up wagon on Rawhide Creek to rodeo in Cody. Todd is now boss of the Pitchfork Ranch where they once were saddle-hands.

1956

Portraits and the large realistic work, *The Italian Bar*. Wyoming for 6 months;
First figurative exhibition, at Martha Jackson Gallery, New York. Life Magazine (July 9) publishes 9 pages on Harry Jackson "Painter Striving to Find Himself" about moving from Abstract on to Realist art. Breaks painting arm at Meeteetse Rodeo, stops bronc riding.

1957

To Italy with Fulbright and Italian government grants. Lives in Florence. Talks with Robert Coe about heroic paintings for Whitney Museum in Cody.

1958

In Pietrasanta, Vignali-Tommasi Foundry, learns to sculpt. First bronzes as studies for *Range Burial* and *Stampede* murals.

1959

Folkways presents album of traditional music called "Harry Jackson, the Cowboy, His Songs, Ballads and Brag Talk" - recognized as definitive work, becomes a collectors' item.

1960

J. Frank Dobie invites him and friend John Graves to Austin, buys 3 bronzes. One-man show

of Western bronzes and drawings at Knoedler's, New York, almost sold out. "Time" May 30th, "Go West Again, Young Man." Meets Peter Hurd, become friends.

1961

Builds studio workshop and house in Camaiore, Italy. Given one-man show, Amon Carter Museum, Fort Worth, Texas. Meets Thomas Hart Benton at artist's home in Kansas City, Mo.; sees the Truman Mural and its painted sculptural models.

1962

September 28, marries Sarah Frothingham Mason, of Westport, Conn. The couple, with their son Matthew, born Italy 1966, live and work permanently in Italy. Return to Wyoming each year.

1963

His bronze monument of Italian folk poet-singer Sor Capanna, unveiled in Piazza dei Mercanti, Rome. Paul Manship befriends and sponsors him for National Sculpture Society. Finishes painting *Range Burial*.

1964

Range Burial central work in major One-man shows at Kennedy Galleries, New York, National Collection of Fine Arts, Washington, D.C., and Whitney Museum of Western Art, Cody, Wyoming. Keynote speaker Annual Convention, Wyoming Art Association. Commissioned to do *River, Road and Point* mural for Pittsburgh. Establishes own foundry in Italy adjacent to studio.

1965

Begins extensive research of French Indian War for Fort Pitt Mural. Thomas Hart Benton demonstrates his methods while visiting Jackson's Italian studio. They tour Italy examining the great murals. "American Artist," November issue, "The *Range Burial*, a Monumental Canvas."

U. S. Marine Corps photo

Marine Sgt. Jackson on Saipan, July 1944.

U. S. Marine Corps Archives

Combat art: Ink drawing of fellow Marine in action, Roi-Namur, 1944.

1966

Completes painting the *Stampede*. *Range Burial* and *Stampede* murals shown together for first time in one-man show, National Cowboy Hall of Fame, Oklahoma City.

1967

"American Heritage," October issue "Death on the Range".

1968

Awarded Gold Medals, National Academy of Design, and Pennational Show. A specially dedicated Pony Express bronze presented to the State of Wyoming. Governor and Mrs. Hathaway honor the artist and Mrs. Jackson with a reception at the governor's mansion. Second one-man show, Amon Carter museum, Fort Worth. Elected fellow, American Artists Professional League.

1969

Stampede and *Range Burial* murals permanently installed for the grand openining of the new Buffalo Bill Museum, Cody, Wyoming. Scheduled installation of mural, Fort Pitt Museum, Pittsburgh.

1970

Scheduled installation of monumental sculpture of Lord Cochrane, Valdivia, Chile; the maritime liberator of Chile, Peru, Brazil and Greece.

One-man Exibitions

1952
Tibor de Nagy Gallery, New York

1953
Tibor de Nagy Gallery, New York

1956
Martha Jackson Gallery, New York

1960
M. Knoedler & Co., New York

1961
Brooklyn Museum, Brooklyn, New York

1961-62
Amon Carter Museum, Fort Worth, Texas

1964
Kennedy Galleries, New York
National Collection of Fine Arts, Washington D.C.
Whitney Gallery of Western Art, Cody, Wyoming
Montana Historical Society, Helena, Montana

1965
Mile High Center, Denver, Colorado

1966
National Cowboy Hall of Fame, Oklahoma City, Oklahoma

1968
Kennedy Galleries, New York
Amon Carter Museum, Fort Worth, Texas
Cody County Art League, Cody, Wyoming

1969
Kennedy Galleries, New York

Group Exibitions

1944
Stendahl Gallery, Los Angeles, California

1945
U. S. Marine Corps Combat Art, opened at the Corcoran Gallery of Art, Washington, D.C., was shown at the Museum of Modern Art, New York, The Tate Gallery, London, and many other great museums

1946
Art Association of Los Angeles, California

1948
Norlyst Gallery, New York
Jacques Seligmann, New York
American Federation of Arts Traveling Exhibition, Brooklyn Museum Art School Gallery, Brooklyn, New York

1949
Jacques Seligmann, New York

1950
Studio 35, New York
Kootz Gallery, New York
The New Gallery, New York

1951
Tibor de Nagy Gallery, New York
9th Street Gallery, New York

1952
Tibor de Nagy Gallery, New York

1953
The Stable Gallery, New York
Tibor de Nagy Gallery, New York
Bennington College, Vermont

1954
The Stable Gallery, New York

1959
James Graham Gallery, New York

1961
Pennsylvania Academy of Fine Arts

1962
Hirschel & Adler Galleries, New York
Valley House Galleries, Dallas, Texas

1964
Cummer Gallery of Art, Florida
National Academy of Design, New York

1965
National Academy of Design, New York
Valley House Galleries, Dallas, Texas
Kennedy Galleries, New York

1966
XVII Mostra Internazionale d'Arte, Premio del Fiorino, Florence, Italy
Sporting Gallery, Midoleburg: Virginia

1967
Pennational Artists Annual (Awarded Interstate Gold Medal), Pennsylvania
National Academy of Design, New York

1968
National Academy of Design (Awarded Samuel Finley Breese Morse Gold Medal), New York
American Artists Professional League, Grand National Show, New York
Hammond Museum, North Salem, New York
Convento di S. Lazzaro, Mostra di Arte Moderna, Camaiore, Italy
Kennedy Galleries, New York
Main Place Gallery, Dallas, Texas

1969
Tryon Gallery, London, England

Some Public Collections and Foundations

American Museum to Great Britain, Bath, England
Amon Carter Foundation, Fort Worth, Texas
Buffalo Bill Museum, Cody, Wyoming
W. R. Coe Foundation, New York, New York
Dickinson College, Carlisle, Pennsylvania
Dobie Memorial Collection, University of Texas

Fort Ligonier Museum, Ligonier, Pennsylvania
Fort Pitt Museum, Pittsburgh, Pennsylvania
Glenbow Foundation, Calgary, Alberta, Canada
Harvie Foundation, Calgary, Alberta, Canada
Montana Historical Society, Helena, Montana
R. W. Norton Foundation, Shreveport, Louisana

Riveredge Foundation, Calgary, Alberta, Canada
Shelburne Museum, Shelburne, Vermont
Whitney Gallery of Western Art, Cody, Wyoming
Woolarac Museum, Bartlesville, Oklahoma
Wyoming State Gallery-Museum, Cheyenne.

Some Private Collections

Stanley Adams, Texas / Jacob Anderson, Texas / Ethan Ayer, Massachusetts / Malcolm Baldrige, Connecticut / Frances Phelps Belden, Wyoming / Thomas Hart Benton, Missouri / Lawrence Black, Oregon / Mrs. René Bouché, New York / Mrs. H. H. Brittingham, Texas / John Brittingham, Colorado / Mrs. George Buchanan, Texas / John Bugas, Michigan / John Bunker, Colorado / Mrs. Arthur P. Burns, Oklahoma / The Hon. John H. Burns, Tanzania / Amon Carter, Jr., Texas / Edward J. Churchill, Connecticut / Christopher Clark, Virginia / Mrs. Henry H. R. Coe, Wyoming / The Hon. Robert Coe, France / Continental Oil Company, New York / Christopher Cord, California / Charles Decker, Pennsylvania / Samuel Decker, Wyoming / William De Maris, Wyoming / Jack Dick, Conn. / H. Richard Dietrich, Pennsylvania / Mrs. J. Frank Dobie, Texas / William Doheny, California / David Dominick, Virginia / Olin Dows, Washington, D. C. / Steven Earle, California / Ben Eaton, California / Arthur Emil, New York / R. Y. Empie, Oklahoma / Logan English, Kentucky / Frederick Feldkamp, France / A. B. Fisher, Pennsylvania / John Ford, California / Adam Fremantle, New York / Anne Fremantle, New York / Richard Fremantle, Italy / Kenneth Frost, New York / Emmanuel Ghent, New York / James Graham, New York / John Graves III, Texas / Clement Greenberg, New York / Mrs. Paul Greever, Wyoming / James Griffin, Idaho / Diane Guggenheim, New York / Ralph Hanes, N. Carolina / H. Roland Harriman, New York / Phyllis Harriman, New York / Harold Hinn, Texas / Ellen Grace Jackson, Illinois / Martha Jackson, New York / Prof. Glenn L. Jepsen, New Jersey / Mrs. J. Lee Johnson III, Texas / The Hon. Lyndon B. Johnson, Texas / Alan Kapelner, New York / M. Knoedler & Co., New York / Dean Krackel, Oklahoma / Dr. Joseph Kriegler, New York / Arthur Krim, New York / H. Peter Kriendler, New York / Edward R. Lawrence, New York / Hester Lewis, Florida / James Lewis, Virginia / Robert Lewis, New York / Jacques Lipchitz, Italy / Beverly Livingston, Wyoming / George Lorimer, Italy / Robert Lovejoy, Connecticut / Thomas McMahon Jr., New Jersey / Hugh Maller, Wyoming / L. W. Manning, New Hampshire / Frank Mason, New York / Harding Mason, New York / Mrs. Ernest May, Jr., Wyoming / Richard K. Mellon, Pennsylvania / Richard K. Mellon III, Pennsylvania / John A. Miller, Illinois / Bruce Moore, Washington D.C. / Randolph Moore, Texas / Hanno Mott, New York / Mrs. Breck Moran, Wyoming / Remington Olmsted, Italy / Astolfo Ottolenghi, Italy / George Packer, Italy / Jay Parsons, Wyoming / John Paxton, Texas / Robert E. Peterson, California / Gene Powell, New York / Stuart Preston, New York / Mariano Protto, Italy / The Hon. Frederick Reinhardt, Switzerland / Ivo Ricci, Italy / A. L. Robinson Connecticut / Francis Robinson, New York / Theodore Rosen, Connecticut / John Ryan, Texas / Raymond Ryan, California / John E. Sanford, California / Tatina Sartori, Italy / Neil Sclater-Booth, New York / Scovill Manufacturing C., Connecticut / W.A. Seifert, Pennsylvania / William Shay, Nevada / Raphael Soyer, New York / Franco Spalleti-Trivelli, Italy / Dr. Albert Starr, Oregon / Henry Stein, Colorado / I. Stein, Pennsylvania / Charles Stillman, New York / Robert A. Stranahan, Ohio / J. B. Tissot, England / Calvin Todd, Wyoming / Gloria Vanderbilt, New York / Aldo Vignali, Italy / The Hon. Leonardo Vitetti, Italy / Harry Webb, Vermont / Daniel Welch, Illinois / H. Wellington, New York / Joseph C. Wheeler, Italy / William Winchester, New York / B. L. Wooley Jr., Texas / Rudolf Wunderlich, New York / Dr. Adrian Zorgnotti, New York.

Photocredits
Lee Angle, Fort Worth, Texas
Marcello Bertoni, Florence, Italy
Christopher Bird, Washington D. C.
Lee Bolton, New York
Brenwasser, New York
Hiscock Studios, Cody, Wyoming

Micheal and Barbara Reed, Cross River, New York
Foto Limar, Camaiore, Italy
Jack Richards Studio, Cody, Wyoming
Walter Rosenblum, New Haven, Conn.
John Shiff, New York
U. S. Marine Corps, Official Photo, Pfc. Mattson
Adrian Zorgnotti, New York

Designer:
Andrei+Lecci, Florence, Italy

Printed in Italy by Conti-Tipocolor,
Florence, Italy.
Photo-gravure by Zincotipia Moderna,
Florence, Italy.